THE GREAT ARTISTS

Gustav Klimt

Anjali Raghbeer

Om KIDZ
An imprint of Om Books International

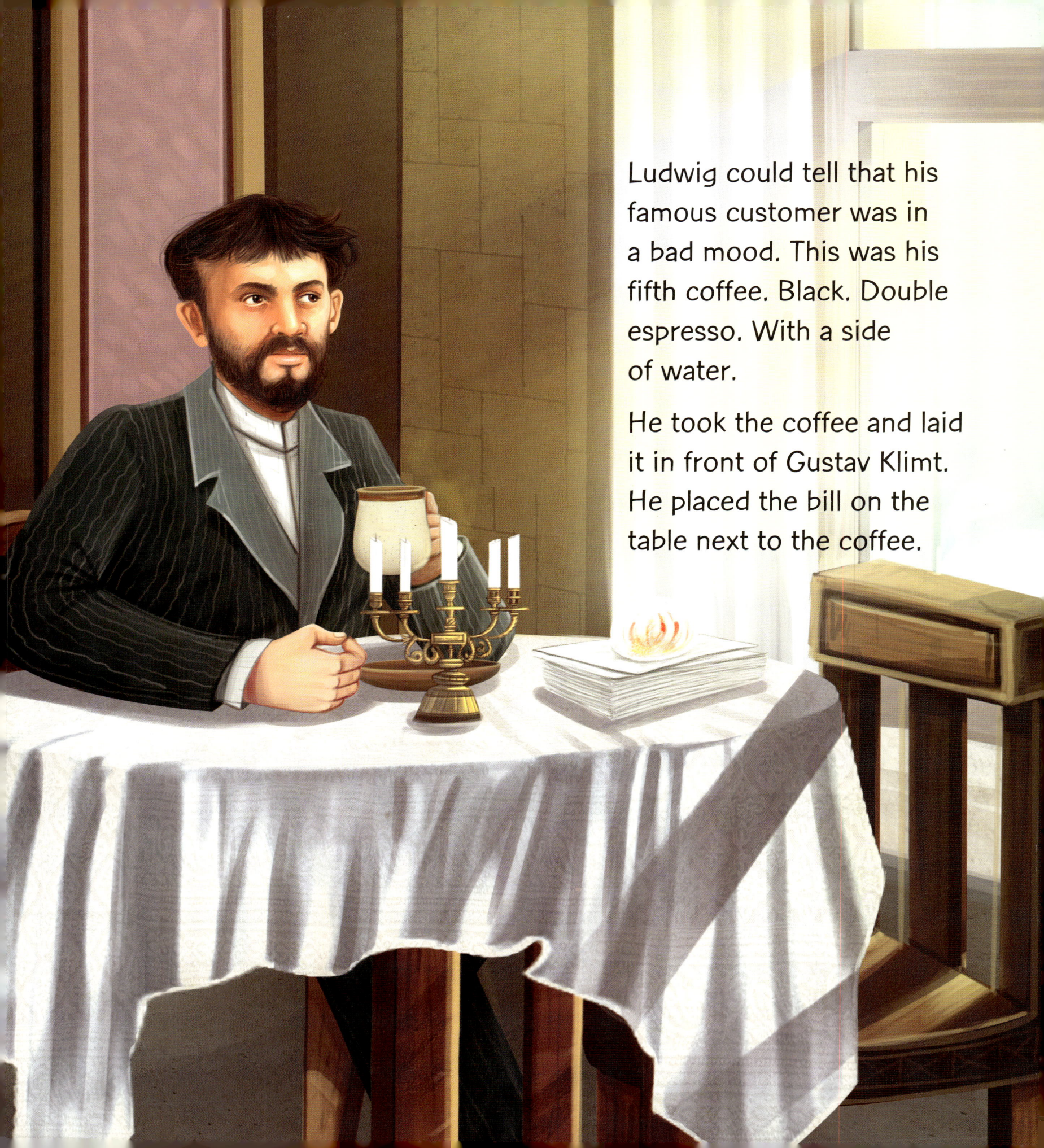

Ludwig could tell that his famous customer was in a bad mood. This was his fifth coffee. Black. Double espresso. With a side of water.

He took the coffee and laid it in front of Gustav Klimt. He placed the bill on the table next to the coffee.

'Sir, will that be all for today?' asked Ludwig.

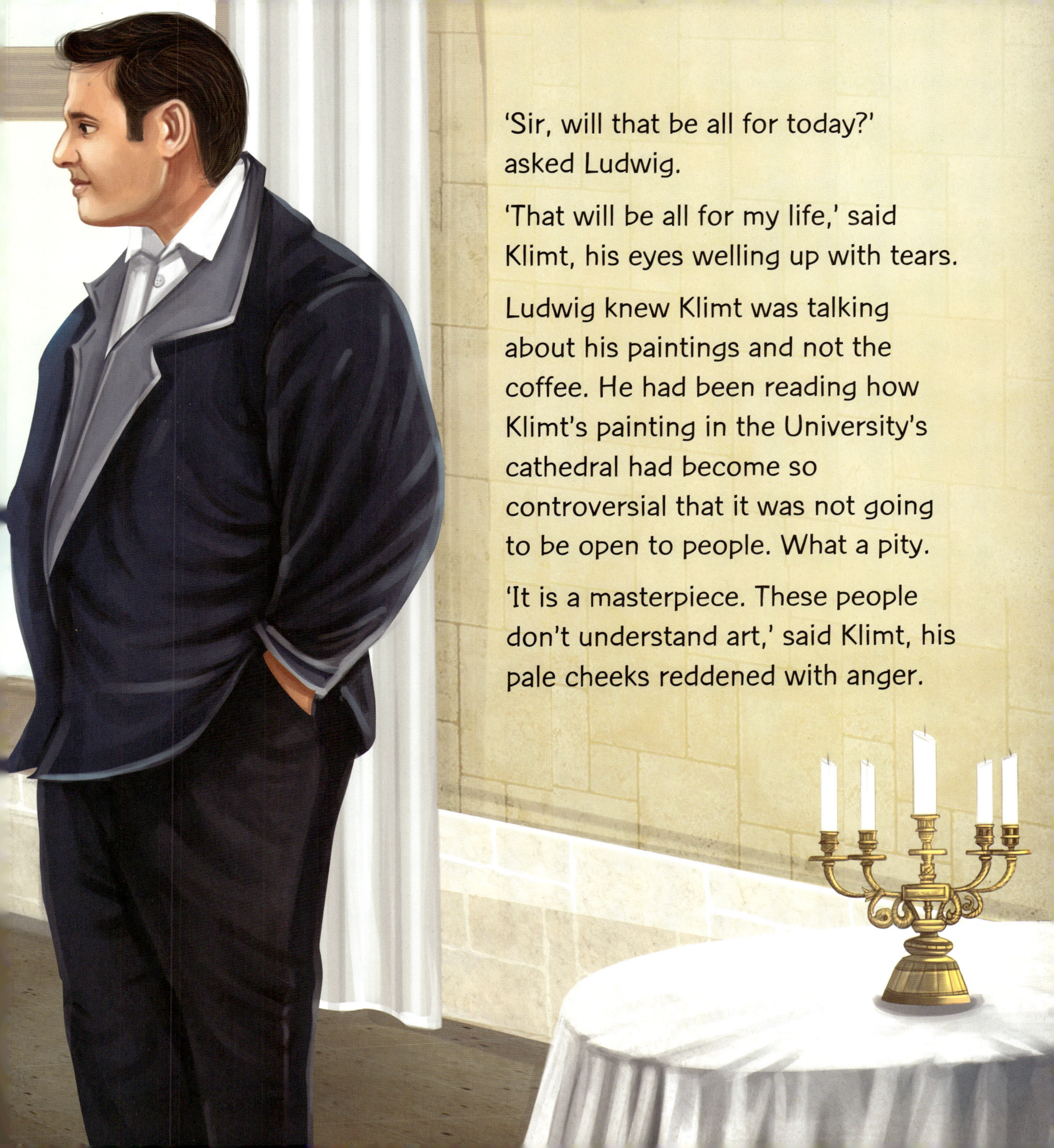

'That will be all for my life,' said Klimt, his eyes welling up with tears.

Ludwig knew Klimt was talking about his paintings and not the coffee. He had been reading how Klimt's painting in the University's cathedral had become so controversial that it was not going to be open to people. What a pity.

'It is a masterpiece. These people don't understand art,' said Klimt, his pale cheeks reddened with anger.

The next week, Klimt was back again. This time he was in a more cheerful mood, noted Ludwig.

'Ferdinand, I want you to meet the man who saved me,' said Klimt to his guest as Ludwig brought them their coffees.

'Yes,' said Klimt. Ludwig looked around. *Me?*

It was then that Ludwig noticed the astonishingly beautiful lady seated next to Ferdinand.

'Adele, you will be immortal,' said Klimt.

'It's settled then, you will paint Adele for our anniversary gift to her parents,' said Ferdinand.

'On one condition,' said Klimt.

'Go ahead.'

'You will let me do it my way,' said Klimt. 'Enough of censorship.'

'I want to get away....I have refused every form of support from the state, I'll do without all of it. It has to be my way.'

Ludwig removed the paper napkins to find that Klimt had drawn sketches of Adele. The tiny white sheets were full of pencil drawings.

Ludwig thought of all the women that Klimt had sketched in his coffee shop. But none had been as beautiful as Adele.

Adele and Klimt came regularly to the café. Adele patiently sat in a chair while Klimt sketched her from various angles.

Ludwig would barely even notice them at times. They became part of the furniture.

But Ludwig wondered how Adele didn't get bored. She had to sit still for two, sometimes three, hours. He knew he couldn't have done it.

He kept each paper napkin that Klimt threw away.

When Adele left, Ludwig shut the café and sat with Klimt.

'I love women,' confessed Klimt, 'They are so beautiful.'

Ludwig had heard rumours that Adele and Ferdinand had been fighting. She was spending too much time with Klimt who was known to fall in and out of love with his models.

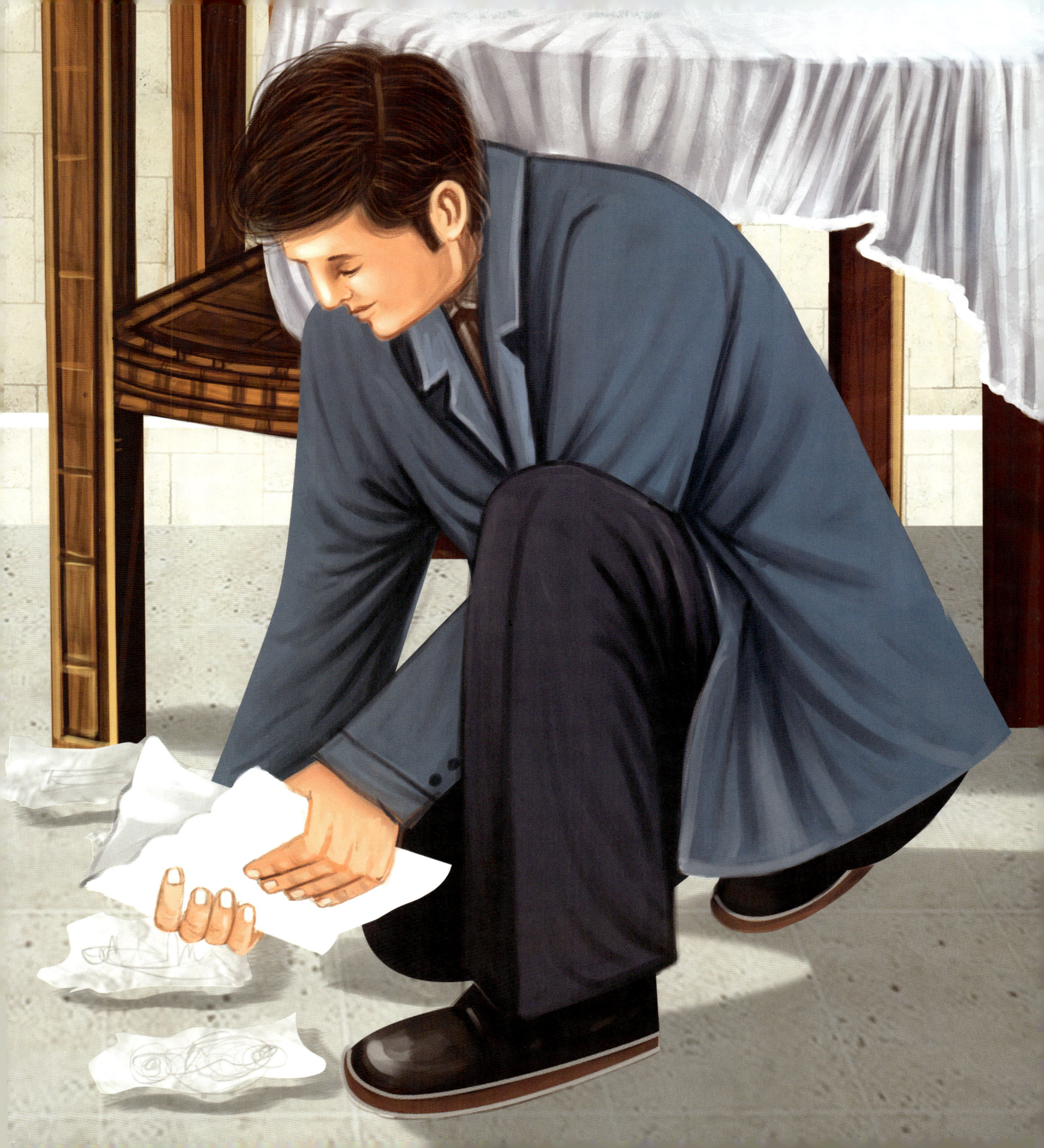

When Klimt didn't come to the café, Ludwig got worried.

One week went. Two weeks went. Three weeks.

Has he fallen ill?

Has he moved out of Vienna?

*Or..oh my God...*Ludwig dared not even think it. *Was he dead?*

Klimt hadn't missed a day in the last seventy-eight days.

Ludwig closed his shop early that day and set off for Klimt's house.

As Ludwig entered Klimt's cottage, Feldmühlgasse Number 11, he saw Klimt's cat perched in the corner.

She went into another room. Soon Klimt came out holding the cat.

It was as if she had told him that Ludwig had come.

'Ludwig, my friend,' said Klimt. He was clad in a robe. His beard had grown long and he looked like he hadn't slept for days.

'I just wanted to see if you are okay,' said Ludwig, feeling awkward now that Klimt seemed perfectly fine.

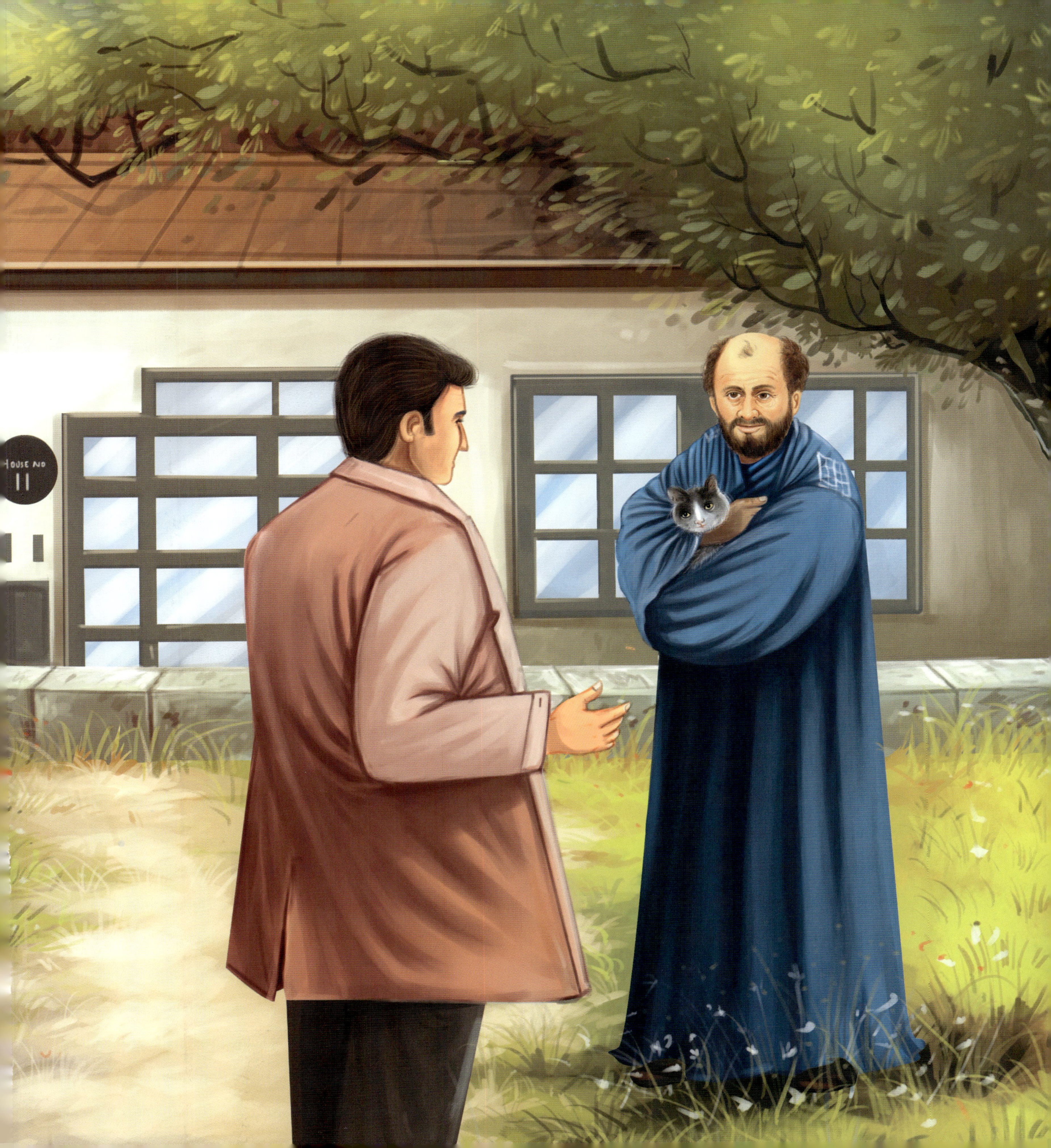
HOUSE NO
11

'I have found gold,' said Klimt.

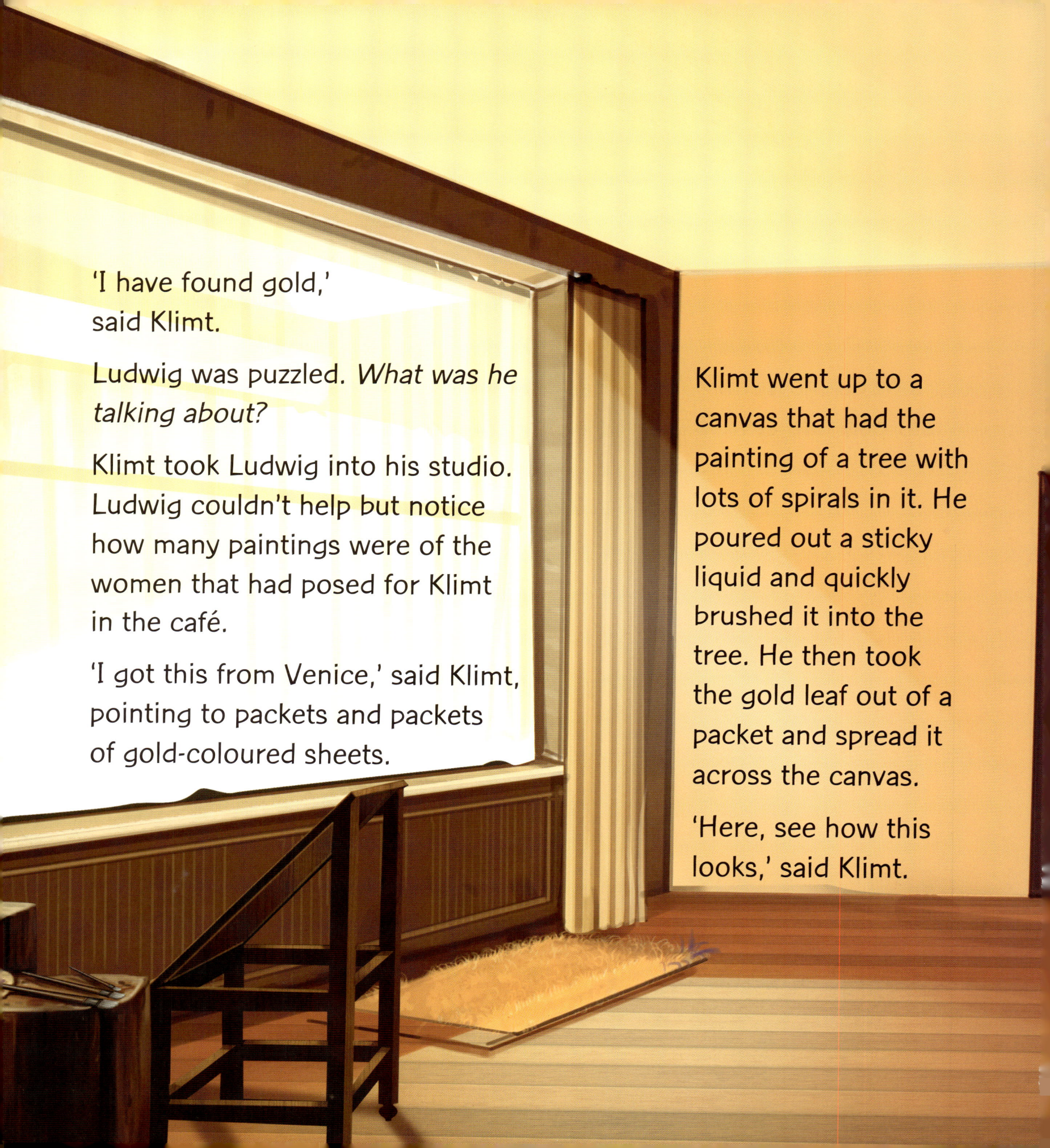

Ludwig was puzzled. *What was he talking about?*

Klimt took Ludwig into his studio. Ludwig couldn't help but notice how many paintings were of the women that had posed for Klimt in the café.

'I got this from Venice,' said Klimt, pointing to packets and packets of gold-coloured sheets.

Klimt went up to a canvas that had the painting of a tree with lots of spirals in it. He poured out a sticky liquid and quickly brushed it into the tree. He then took the gold leaf out of a packet and spread it across the canvas.

'Here, see how this looks,' said Klimt.

A golden hue surrounded the tree. It was magical.

'The Tree of Life,' said Klimt.

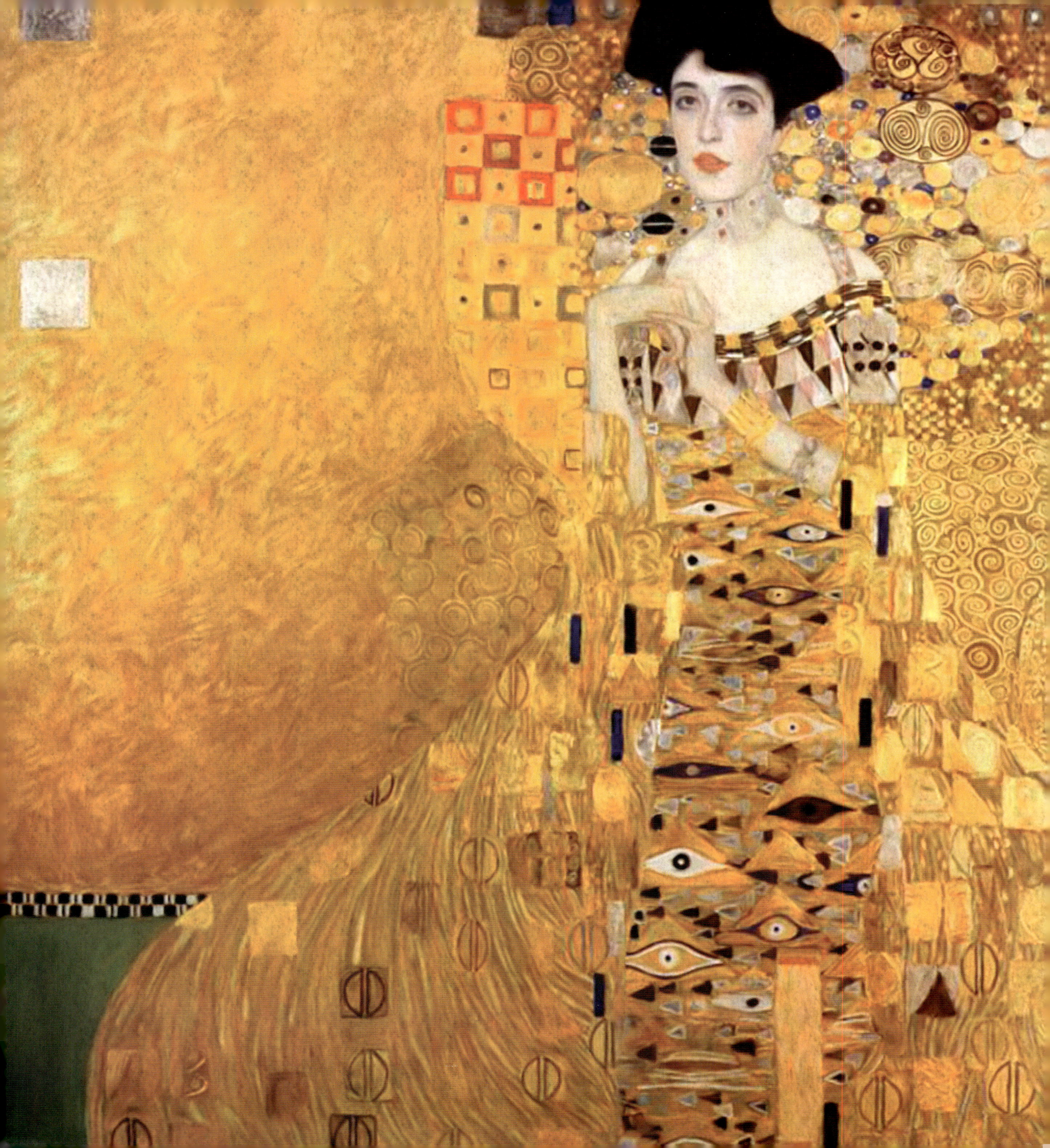

It was getting late; Ludwig had been so fascinated by Klimt's paintings that he had forgotten the time.

The doorbell rang.

Adele entered the room, she was looking even more beautiful this evening.

'I must get going, Sir,' said Ludwig.

'Nonsense,' said Klimt, 'Stay. See how the painting is coming along.'

Klimt adjusted Adele to pose for the painting.

Ludwig was speechless. The painting was even more striking than the lady.

'What are these eyes in the painting?' asked Ludwig.

'In the Byzantine paintings, they use symbols. Her beauty is protected from the evil eye,' said Klimt. 'The old and the new must exist side by side.'

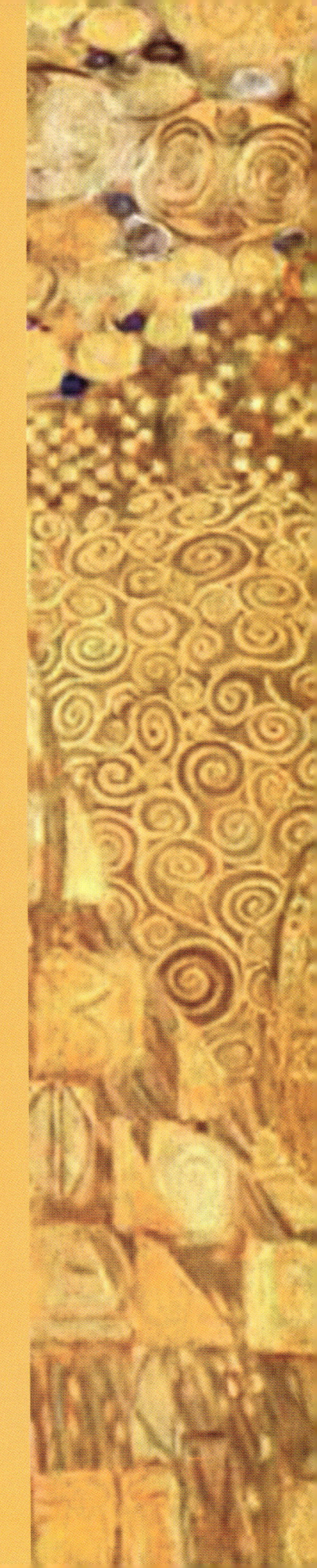

Klimt came less and less to the café. Ludwig guessed he had become very busy with his work.

One morning, Klimt burst into the café. Ludwig had never seen Klimt so excited.

'They want my paintings again,' said Klimt. 'Ludwig, if you hadn't told me to believe in myself, I would have given up.'

Ludwig smiled.

Klimt showed him a painting that he had in his large art folder.

'The Kiss,' said Klimt. 'People will remember me for it, Ludwig.'

Ludwig got Klimt his favourite coffee as Klimt sketched once again on Café Museum's paper napkin.

Gustav Klimt was born on 14 July 1862 in Vienna, Austria.

His father was a gold engraver who had migrated from Bohemia, while his mother aspired to become a professional musician.

At the age of 14 he won a full scholarship to study at the Vienna School of Arts & Crafts.

In 1883, Gustav opened a studio, *Company of Artists*, with his brother and a friend, Franz Masch.

In 1888, the studio received the Golden Order of Merit from Austro-Hungarian Emperor Franz Josef I for their outstanding work.

In 1890, the studio joined the Vienna Artists' association.

In 1897, Klimt resigned from the Vienna Artists' association to found the Vienna Secession. This group was more non-traditional and believed in bringing international shows to Vienna.

In the 1900s, Klimt's paintings have been often described as his Golden Phase because of his extensive use of the gold leaf and Byzantine mosaics.

In 1918, Gustav fell ill at the age of 55, and died on 16 February..

His most famous paintings are often stated to be, 'The Kiss' and 'Portrait of Adele Bloch-Bauer I'.